T0063013

CHARLIE'S WAVE

Charlie De La Cruz

BALBOA.
PRESS

A DIVISION OF HAY HOUSE

Balboa Press books may be ordered through booksellers or by contacting:

Balboa Press
A Division of Hay House
1663 Liberty Drive
Bloomington, IN 47403
www.balboapress.com
1 (877) 407-4847

Printed in the United States of America.

ISBN: 978-1-4525-1634-9 (sc)
ISBN: 978-1-4525-1635-6 (e)

Balboa Press rev. date: 06/13/2014

This book has been in my heart for many years. I felt by telling my story I could share with the world how I overcame a difficult and painful past to embrace a beautiful and magical life. I now know anyone who has the desire to move through and past the pain has the opportunity to live heaven on earth. Every time one more person steps up to the plate and actively heals their soul the entire world heals a little bit more. Life is free choice. A journey that we choose. I have chosen my path every step of the way. This is my journey and by writing this book I am praying it helps you on your journey, your truth, and your beautiful life. God Bless :)

Contents

Early Life: Sunshine and Fun

When I was a little girl I loved running through the woods barefoot, playing in the creek, exploring the beautiful plants, trees, and animals. It was my favorite place to be. Nothing seemed impossible. My siblings and I were allowed to play near our home throughout the summer months as long as we came home at supper time. My mom would whistle so loud that I am sure the kids in the next neighborhood heard it too. My summer months were spectacular. My brother Mark loves animals. He caught and trained mice to do tricks. He brought home baby rabbits and we attempted to raise them. The day he brought home the momma bat with nine babies attached to her my mom flipped. She said he had to put it back where he found it.

I enjoyed visiting the Nun who lived near us. She made pies for the church and she always made cinnamon crisp for me out of the extra pie crust. She gave me a beautiful pink rosary and I was in awe over the beauty of this magical necklace. I was so young but I knew she had given me a gift from her heart. She said it would protect me. It did. Shortly after she had given me the rosary I knocked on her door. A stranger opened the door and told me the church had moved the Nun to a different location. I was sad to know that my wonderful friend had moved. The Nun and I had become good friends and I believe her prayers and rosary protected me and are quite possibly still protecting me today. She was my first friend and I loved her. 0:)

My other memories from early childhood were wonderful. I remember waking up on Christmas and opening presents. My sister Brenda and I loved playing and jumping around the house in those darn leotards. My family was intact. I thought my older brother, Mark, could do no wrong. When my little brother, Joe, was about 2 years old, Brenda and I dressed him up as a girl and introduced him as our cousin, Joann, to the entire neighborhood. He is still traumatized to this day about that little adventure, but it was so much fun. It was like having a live doll and I remember him being so happy that his big sisters were paying attention to him. He didn't mind the makeup, necklaces, or the pretty dress that he was wearing. Priceless. Great memories.

Dark Horizons

Dark times landed in the walls of my home shortly after that, and somehow, in some way, I was protected from the worst of it. Even now, writing about it makes me so sad. It was so tragic and frightening for a little girl. I first remember my parents physically fighting in the hallway of our home. It was late at night and the noise awoke my brother, sister, and I. My big brother, Mark, tried to break it up and the police were called. My Dad was a police officer at that time so the whole situation was brushed under the rug. My Dad was drinking a lot as the marriage was beginning to break down. One night I heard yelling and doors slamming. I looked for my Mother and I thought she was in the bathroom. I knocked on the door crying to be let in because I was scared. I turned around and my Dad was holding his police revolver and pointing it at my head. I knew he was intoxicated because he was swaying back and forth. I do not remember what he said to me but I knew my life may end right at that very moment. My Mother was not in the bathroom. She had climbed out the window and had gone to a friend's house. I just remember silently walking back to my bedroom in shock and heartbroken that my sweet Dad would shoot me. Shortly after this incident my Dad and his buddy, Fred, decided to hold up a diner. Dad used his police revolver in the burglary. Fred must have gotten scared so he took off in the getaway car. My Dad was apprehended with loot in hand walking down the road. He spent the next 2 years in prison and my Mom divorced him.

Around that same time my brother, Mark, met a deacon and a children's bible teacher at our local church. This man was also a first grade teacher. When he was allowed in to our family fold I believe the devil himself walked through our door. He and I despised each other from day one. It is funny how a child can see through a mask, isn't it. After my parents divorced we moved a few times in the following year. We were doing ok but we lacked adult supervision and my big brother took care of us when my Mom was working. I remember seeing the deacon at our new school talking to the principal in the playground one day. The deacon did not live near or teach at our school so there was no reason for him to be buddying up to the principal. Soon I found out why he had made a visit. The principal expelled my brother for being in possession of a cigarette and instead of moving my brother to a new school or moving our household my Mother gave up all rights to my brother and allowed the deacon/ teacher/ pedophile to adopt him. My brother was tortured by this monster the rest of his childhood. On a few occasions the deacon shot a gun at my brother and the bullet ended up in the door above his head. It was meant to control and manipulate my strong and noble brother, and it did. The devil was finally brought to justice about five years ago. For all of those years he was a supposed pillar in his community. He died alone in prison. His mask was finally revealed. I believe the world is now safe from this maniac, but how many beautiful children did he hurt? My heart still cries for my brother. He was not protected. He had no where to go. All four of us kids were without protection in a very scary world. My brother Mark and I communicate today and he has had such a tough life. He has the heart of gold but his past has him trapped in a world of pain and anguish. How does he get out? I write to him and talk to him on the phone and tell him how much I love him. I hope it gives him peace. If and when he can, he will break through the chains that bind him to that horrible past and once again live heaven on earth with me. I cannot make sense out of this horrendous catastrophe. Why did this happen to my wonderful brother. Why did he have to go through all of this pain and suffering? Some heart aches never stop hurting.

My fondest memories of my brother Mark is when we were playing in the woods near our home. He and I loved the woods. We would explore the creek and one of my first memories is of us running along the creek barefoot, happy, and free. At that moment I was the happiest I had ever been. I wanted to be just like my awesome brother. He was honest and noble. He was and will always be my Hero. He caught a snake one day and it bit him on the back. He made me promise not to tell our mother and since he was the coolest brother ever I did not tell. He also took my side whenever my sister and I had an argument. Thank you Mark. I knew you had my back and that meant so much to me. The last magical memory I had before he was taken away by the pedophile was when all four of us kids danced to "Black Water," by the Doobie Brothers. We were so blissfully happy at that moment. Little Joe was only 3 years old. Mark was our protector. My sister and I were so happy in that moment, just singing and dancing in a circle by our dining room windows with the sun shining in on us. I have held on to that memory through all of the hard times and said thank you, thank you, thank you for that moment in time. It was over way too soon. No one can take away the love we have for each other. In that moment we celebrated it before evil set in. He was shipped off to the deacon's house shortly after that. Tears still flow. It is still heartbreaking to go there. I just keep saying, what if and I know I cannot change it but if I could I would re-write our childhood and keep everything the way it was before my parents started really messing up all of our lives.

My parents met in Germany while my father was in the service. My mother is from a small little village in Germany. The day she got the call that my Dad had been arrested for holding up the diner she told us that she was divorcing him. My Dad had been having affairs so the burglary was just the last straw. We moved into an apartment. She worked as a waitress and life was tough but manageable. I missed our old house and friends. I missed my Dad. He was in prison and I remember seeing him in prison on one occasion. He had a beard and mustache and I asked him why he grew it. He said he had arrested some of the guys he was in prison with and he did not want them to recognize him.

As my mom was walking home with a bag full of groceries one day a man offered her a ride home on his motorcycle. She accepted and for the next 2 years our lives were a complete hell. Mom's new boyfriend was a woman/child beater and drug addict. This was about the time my brother was adopted off and the we had no protection from this maniac, gang member, drug abuser. Many nights I woke up to the sound of screaming, crying, pleading, crashing furniture, and my mom's body hitting the floor. Too scared to move, praying that my Mom was alive and finding her beaten and battered the next morning, literally traumatized me. She always told me the door hit her in the face. I knew what had happened to her and I could not understand why she was lying for this piece of shit for a human being. She was completely purple and swollen. I could not recognize her because her injuries were so severe. She did not look like my beautiful mother. I remember thinking she looked like a purple monster. It made me so sad. This was a beaten woman, physically and spiritually. I did not know how to help her. I was devastated. We smelled marijuana and very loud music erupted from our basement. My little brother found needles in my Mom's purse which makes sense because she was always out of it. She looked zoned out most of the time. Our new step Dad was in a band and they played music and partied all night, every night. They were a biker gang and everyone was scared of them. My little brother was afraid to leave his room so he would urinate on his big yellow pillow and then he would get a beating from the new step dad for urinating on the pillow. It was insane how we lived. We had the water and electricity shut off so we did not have clean clothes for school. I was put in the slow learner corner because I was beaten, neglected, traumatized, and barely hanging on at that time. Again an angel found me. She taught my second grade class and she knew that I was in bad shape. She was kind to me and I will never forget her. I won bunny ears during the Easter party that year I believe she was behind it. Those darn bunny ears were nothing to someone else but to a kid barely hanging on they were a gift from heaven. The year we lived with the woman and child abuser I ran away three times. I took my little brother and my big sister with me. The first time we ran to the woods with most of our belongings. We were determined to make a place to live in the ravine, which was somewhat protected by the cold wind. Eventually we became so cold and hungry that we were forced to go home. I remember leaving my belongings in the ravine because I was too cold to collect everything. Home was horrible, scary, dark, and loveless. I hated it there. The sheriff lived next door so I went to his office one day and told him about the abuse going on in our house. He handed me a little bottle of coke and listened intently. Thinking I was going to get some help I began to get optimistic. I felt the nightmare might soon end. After listening he said to me, "The only way I can arrest your step daddy is if he beats your Momma on the front lawn. I cannot go into the home." This was

Arkansas, 1976. What could I expect? Shortly after that conversation with the sheriff my Dad drove by with his new girlfriend. He was not in the picture after going to prison for 2 years so I was surprised to see him. He wrote a number on the bottom of my sister's shoe and told us to call him if we needed him. We needed him right then but again we had no protection. He drove off that day with his new girlfriend and left us in hell. He did take our family dog though. I understand that my Dad would have gone back to prison but knowing what was going on in that home and not trying to get us out of there just stuns me.

Shortly after my Dad left the number on the shoe I woke up to more screaming, crying, crashing, and pain. My Mom was being beaten again. She was pregnant at this time and I was extremely worried about her and the baby. The step Dad had her on the floor by the front door. He was stomping on her extended belly with his hiking boot, trying to kill the baby. My Mom was trying to protect her belly but it did not help. It was a horrific scene. I had crawled from my room to the hallway and I knew if he saw me I would be dead or beaten to a pulp so I could do nothing to help my Mother. I crawled back to my room and cried all night. I devised a plan at that time to try another escape. Early the next morning I climbed out the window of my bedroom and ran to our neighbor's house.

The nice couple let me use their phone and I tried to get in contact with my father. I could not reach him by phone and the neighbors became very nervous that the step dad might discover my absence. They wanted to help us so they called the Department of Human Services and the police department. The sheriff could not ignore my pleas anymore because DHS had been called. {If you ever need help call two agencies because they are now all involved and they check on each other. When I spoke with the sheriff alone there were no witnesses.} As I write this I still feel the relief of finally getting away from this hell that we were forced to live. My two siblings were taken from the home at that point and my Mother was asked to pack some of our belongings. We left that day in the back of a Department of Human Services vehicle. My Mother beaten and battered, cried on my neighbors porch and I had to look down at my lap so I wouldn't see her cry anymore. I love her and I did not want to leave her but I had to try to save my sister, brother, and myself. She had to decide if she was going to stay or leave this hell she was living. I was only 8 years old at that time but I knew that this monster we lived with would have killed us had we stayed in that home.

I do not know what goes through the mind of someone who stays in an abusive relationship. I did find out years later that she was beaten by her step father when she was a little girl in Germany so maybe it set a life pattern in place. I do not know. I just could not understand it. Was it the drug abuse or addiction that made her stay? I just know 4 children were at the mercy of this woman who did not protect them. I just do not understand how you can see your children being beaten, neglected, cast aside and do nothing. This person is not well. This is my nicest explanation. She watched and did nothing when my brother was beaten. She watched and did nothing when I was beaten. My brother was only 4 years old. He was just a baby. We had no one to protect us.

The Good, the Bad and the Ugly

My sister, brother, and I ended up in a small town in Arkansas. A preacher and his wife fostered us. Within the first 4 months of us living in our new home my eye sight deteriorated. I remember sitting across the room watching television shortly after we moved to the foster home. By the 3rd to 4th month my foster Mom noticed I was sitting directly in front of the television and mentioned it to me. I hadn't noticed how my eyes were changing but it did happen almost overnight. I was fitted for glasses and they were a very high prescription. Witnessing my Mother being stomped on and beaten the night before I ran again might have a lot to do with my eye sight deteriorating so quickly. We lived on a farm and our life revolved around church. I liked the preacher but did not care for his wife very much. Yes, I was grateful to be out of the hell that we had come from but the preacher's wife was determined to beat the spirit out of my little brother. She used switches and for

Christmas he received lumps of coal and switches from the tree outside the front door. My little brother was a very beaten little boy. The foster Mom took him to every psychologist she could find. They would observe this little guy and be absolutely mortified at his actions. My brother had been beaten and left in his room for 2 years. How did they expect him to be. I could not protect him and I did not know what to do.

We did have some good times on the farm. We were there when the calf was born. She was so beautiful. I picked up the eggs in the hen house and I had to run really fast so the chickens would not peck at my ankles. We had milk from the cow but I so repulsed by the cream that floated on the milk. I learned how to scoop the cream off the milk and used a ladle to get to the good stuff. It was delicious. We had a revival in the woods and to three kids this was a huge event. We were so excited and the energy was amazing. My siblings and I were scheduled to sing "It's Bubblin," at the revival. We stood on stage and started to sing. I looked at my brother and started smiling. He started laughing and we proceeded to laugh uncontrollably until they asked us to step down off the stage. The preacher and the wife never asked to sing again. They were so mad at us. We had embarrassed them in front of their congregation. When my brother and I get together we can still make each other laugh to the point of tears and I love him so much. I just wish I could have protected him back then. He never deserved the abuse he received at the hands of these adults.

My dad was remarried after we had been in foster care for a year so we went to live with him and his new wife. About three weeks into this new situation my Dad came home intoxicated and the new wife told him to take us back to foster care because she was leaving him so he did. It was the longest ride of my life. I was so sad sitting in the back seat of that car while my own Dad took us back to foster care. I will never forget it but I am trying to forgive it. The Lord had a reason for all of this pain and the person I am and the person I am becoming has broken through the chains of hell and pain on this earth. I write this as the tears still fall and the healing continues.

After our Dad delivered us to the Department of Human Services we lived with a different couple and their two daughters in another small town in Arkansas. My brother was once again beaten and by this time he just expected it. I stumbled upon the foster parent's weakness one time and used it to our advantage as much as I could. They were being mean to my brother so I told them to take us back to Department of Human Services. They became sugary sweet and "talked" me into not calling DHS. I used that threat a number of times but it did not completely protect my brother from the black eyes and beatings he received. My foster Mother arrived home 2 hours after we returned home from school and we were ordered to sit at the table and study until she arrived home. My grades skyrocketed and by fifth grade I was voted the smartest girl in the class. I enrolled in band and played basketball and softball. The sports and music were a gift. My foster parents came to every event and cheered me on. I excelled at that time and I believe it was because I had the support of my foster parents. We lived with them for 3 years and in 1980 we were given the choice to visit our Mother in Idaho.

My Mom had gotten rid of the maniac step Dad 1 year after we were placed in foster care. It took her a total of 4 years to get us back. At that time I refused to visit my Dad or my Mom. I felt that I should not have to say goodbye to my own parents so why should I say hello. My Dad was very hurt by this and I was at the point that I did not care. I was so heartbroken at seeing them leave me after a 2 hour visit that it was less painful not to see them at all. When the DHS worker met with us and informed us that my mother wanted us to visit her in Idaho I refused. She met with me a few times and finally convinced me to visit by telling me that if I had any problems at my mother's house I could call her immediately and she would pick me up and bring me back to Arkansas. That satisfied me and I finally agreed to a visit. The Department of Human Services actually put the three of us on a bus without adult supervision en route to Idaho. I wonder if DHS still puts foster kids on buses alone.

Shadowed Adolescence

When we arrived in Idaho I looked for my Mother out the window of the bus and could not find her. When I did see her I was shocked. My beautiful Mother looked different. Beat up by life she did not look the same. On the outside she looked very similar but on the inside I could feel the pain, darkness, sadness, and heartache that still clung to her once shining and spunky spirit. We were so happy to meet our little sister the night we arrived at my Mother's home. She was born healthy considering the fact that she had been stomped on when my Mother was pregnant with her. She carries the permanent marks on her body today. Her back and arms turn purple when she gets cold. The skin did not form perfectly but she is alive. She has had health issues her entire life but considering what I witnessed the night before I ran, she is doing well. When we came home she was just 4 years old. She was cute as a button and smart as a whip. She really is a miracle baby. It took a very strong little soul to survive what she went through and I give her so much credit for her will to live. I wish I could say life was perfect and we all lived happily ever after but some stories don't always end as the curtain falls.

After my little brother, big sister, and I arrived at my Mother's we had the decision to stay with her if we wanted too. We all decided to stay with our Mother and it was better is some ways but very heartbreaking in other ways. She lived in an apartment and it was too small for all of us so she rented the apartment across the hall from her. My older sister, my younger brother, and I shared the new apartment. My Mom, my little sister and my Mom's new boyfriend, Ed, lived in the apartment across the hall. This might have worked well because there were only two doors between us but many nights my 2 siblings and I were locked out of my Mom's apartment because she didn't want to deal with us. We would knock and my mom and Ed just ignored us. My little brother was just 8 years old at that time. My mom's boyfriend has never hidden the fact that he did not want us around so my last 6 years at home were spent feeling unwanted, abused, and unloved. We were treated like dirt. Food was cooked, clothes were clean. This is what I remember. No love, just people that did not want us. They drank every other night, like clockwork. Coming home was very tough.

The years of my early youth were so far away. Just a dim memory remained. It was like a whispering dream of a day when we had a beautiful home, wonderful parents that loved us, and joyous times. I just had to deal with it. My little brother was not getting beaten with switches anymore. My sister had a job and a nice boyfriend. I played sports and flute for my 7th, 8th, and 9th grade but I stopped excelling at anything. No one was there to encourage me anymore. No one came to my games. No one cared. It hurt to be the only kid on the team that did not have a parent there to cheer them on. I finally let all of the extra-curricular activities go by 10th grade I turned to alcohol by 8th grade and drugs by 10th grade. Here is an excerpt from my 1981 diary. "Tonight has been terrible. It started when Mom dropped Tori and I off at Linda's (my childhood friends). We then went up to the arcade. When Mom called Linda's I wasn't there but Jack (Linda's brother) was, and he did not give me the message that Mom had called. When I got home mom yelled at me and slapped me and pulled my hair. She even called me a whore and a slut. I was walking out of the room when Mom said if I leave I am not ever coming back. She yelled some more and I have been crying ever since. PLEASE GOD HELP ME." I just ran across this excerpt 3 days ago. It breaks my heart for that little girl. I called my Mom and read it to her. I remember her slapping me in high school but for some reason the pain of this particular incident was so devastating that my mind blocked it and I had no idea this happened to me so young. I remember her doing this to my older sister and pulling her down the stairs by her hair. On that particular evening I ran to our neighbor's house with my sister and we slept on their couch that night. Why do I tell you this now? Secrets have plummeted my family into the brink of hell and I just refuse to have the secrets linger anymore. My beautiful siblings have suffered enough and I not only tell the world my story I tell it for them too. It is truly amazing that we are alive today. From here we heal. My mother no longer gets a front row seat to my life. When I called her the other day, crying as I read this entry she just said, "I don't remember that." Well of course she does not remember, she was drunk out of her mind half of the time. She does not remember the monster she becomes when she is intoxicated. I said, "I do not remember this particular incident, but I do remember you waiting for me in the dark one night when I was in high school. When I walked in the kitchen you slapped me across the face, yelled at me, and called me horrible names. I would never hit my own Mother back, out of respect. How dare you, how dare you, how dare you," and then I hung up. She never called back. That pretty much sums it all up, right. Some things do not change in 33 years, like secrets and denial. I look back and it was truly insane how we lived. I was in survival mode all of those years so I would wait until all of the lights would go out in our home before I came in. I knew she would be passed out and she would not get the chance to abuse me that night. By the morning we always had our unloving Mom back but at least she wasn't a monster in the morning. Survival does funny things, doesn't it? Insanity was what we lived with and it is all we had at that time.

As if I did not have enough problems at home I had middle school to deal with. Our school was in the worst neighborhood and I learned a very valuable lesson early on. I was bullied because I was the new girl and I suppose I looked like an easy target. I was an ugly duckling. Stick thin, my hair was cut short and I had a really bad perm. To top it off I had huge thick glasses that I got teased about all of the time. 5 girls taunted and bullied me constantly for those first few months and I was scared all the time. I did not know what to do or where to go for help. The school was empty one afternoon and I was in the 1st floor bathroom. The girls began harassing me again and I had enough crap to deal with in my life to let these girls intimidate me anymore. I slammed my books on the floor so hard and so loud that it sounded like an explosion and the windows shook. The girls may have thought I had a gun. All of my anger, hurt, pain, sadness, and heartache came out and I was determined to take them all on and if I went down they were coming with me. They backed down and they NEVER EVER bothered me again. From that day forward it was, "Hi Charlie, how are you?" Funny what life hands you sometimes. I also lived in a rough part of town and I was a minority in my neighborhood so I learned to walk with confidence and I put my hands in my jacket all the time so it looked like I had a weapon. Eventually I bought a butterfly knife and nun chucks and learned how to use them. I looked people in the eye when they were walking toward me and I never got harassed again. With drug dealers, thieves, and prostitutes living next door I was allowed to live in peace and I will always appreciate that. They left me alone and I left them alone. In the midst of outlaws there was a discreet respect for each other and we minded our own business. All of us.

The only time I was threatened was when I was walking home from school one day. I walked by a house and this big fat white guy came out the door and was standing there in his underwear. He said, "Come here little girl." I ran to my house so fast. That scared me but I did not know that I could turn this piece of crap in. Would the police department help me in 1981? Who knows. I just walked a different way home from school after that.

Life carried on and we moved to an actual house in a better neighborhood by the time I was in 10th grade. I worked a lot in high school as a fast food employee. It most likely kept me out of trouble. It was an easy time. I did not excel in school anymore and I am not sure if I actually legally had the grades to pass. They did end up graduating me so I did walk across the stage, though. We partied a lot in high school. My friends and I just didn't care about too much at that time. Some of us stuck together and avoided home because home was not a loving or healthy place to be. We hung out at the park near our homes that had a huge hill with picnic tables and a shelter. We played Frisbee and hacky sack and did that teenager hang out thing. Yes there was alcohol and pot at times. My friend, Josh, was going on a beer run and had a few people in his jeep one day. He asked me to buy beer because I had a fake ID. I was getting ready to leave with them but for some reason, at the last moment, I did not go. Another group of us left shortly after that in another car. We were all heading to the same convenience store because "Brown Eyes" would always sell us beer, even though he knew we were underage. We ended up witnessing the aftermath of my friend flipping his jeep. He was unconscious in the middle of the road and the other two guys in the jeep ran off. I ran over to him and yelled to onlookers to call the cops. I sat next to him in the middle of the street until the police and ambulance arrived. He was unconscious the whole time and I did not know if he would even live. I spoke to him and I wondered if he could hear me. He ended up going to the hospital and recovering with a permanent scar on his cheek but otherwise ok. It wasn't a horrible scar. Just a reminder of how close he came to ending it all that day. He had been flipped from the jeep because seat belt laws had not been passed yet. Had the boys been seat belted that day they may have been crushed under the jeep as it flipped. I also thanked God that day that I had not gotten in the jeep. I have not spoken to Josh for many years and I hope he is living a beautiful life. After the accident we spoke about it. I told him what I saw that day and that I was with him until police arrived. He thanked me for being there for him. I am sure he had such a tough time after that incident but he only said he learned so much and he was grateful to be alive. Sweet angelic soul in that boy.

When times were rough as a youngster I just had this calm feeling that if I could just make it to the age of 18 my life would finally be mine and I could create the future that I envisioned. Because of my past I did not trust or like adults very well. Not being able to have any say about my life felt very out of control and scary. God help me. I literally had no where to turn at that time in my life. I had already seen the foster parents get away with beating my brother and I. Foster care wasn't a choice for me and being at home was just as dangerous. I learned to avoid Jekyl and Hyde when I could. I was home only when I had to be. This was my strategy. Even though my home life was insane, loveless and cold, my friends saved me. They were my glue. They had no idea what I had been through or what I was dealing with at home, but they had my back. Thank you!!!! So many people helped me see love, kindness, laughter, and fun, I will forever and ever be grateful. If they need me anytime, anywhere, anyway, I will be here for them. They never knew I was a kid suffering from post-trauma, foster care, abuse, neglect, and that I resided in a hellish alcoholic home and they were my saving grace. I am so blessed to have them in my life. I get to see my old friends on Face Book now and it warms my heart. I cry when they cry, I feel joy for them when they have wonderful milestones in their lives and I send them blessings, love, and compassion. These are some of the most wonderful people I have ever met. 7 months ago I pulled out my old photo album and began posting high school and junior high photos. I carried a camera with me all the time in those days so I have hundreds of photos. My friends were just amazed and over joyed that I had caught our shenanigans on film. I am so happy to remind them of what fun we had. God Bless my dear friends. I Love You.

Beginning the Awakening

After graduating high school I held a number of jobs. I was a waitress, restaurant manager, Insurance agent, I leased office equipment, and after my first son was born I had a daycare in my home for two years. My son was very sick at that time and the only way to keep the symptoms at bay were to give him albuterol treatments, antibiotics, cough medicine and steroids. He was admitted to the hospital at least 5 times from birth to 18 months. Nothing cured my son until I brought him to a Chiropractor. He adjusted my son and my son never required medicine again. My son has been antibiotic free for 20 years. I was 26 at the time and whatever the Chiropractor had done for my son was a miracle to me. I wanted to help people the way my son had been helped. Since my grades were less than average in high school I felt I would not be accepted into a Chiropractic college but I decided to apply anyway. Lo and behold a Chiropractic College accepted my application. I made the big decision to go for my dreams and many people around me were not happy about it. They were happy with me being the way I was. I wasn't. At the time I made the decision to commit to a seven year medical program I was married with a two year old. I did not have very much confidence in myself and I was scared to death. What if I failed? What if I just couldn't cut it in school? Many doubts plagued me. Through the fear and doubt, I went for it anyway. At this time I had been out of high school for 8 years. What did I have to show for it? I felt that going for something amazing, life changing, and extremely difficult was a whole lot better than just puttering around aimlessly for the next 7 years. Well I began undergrad shortly after making the decision to follow my dreams and a year later my family and I moved to Georgia so I could pursue my degree.

My ex-husband and I were such good friends. We laughed and joked with each other all of the time. We cared deeply for each other and I will always appreciate him for loving me unconditionally. Unfortunately the tradeoff was that I was expected to put up with the insanity of living with an alcoholic again. Maybe I picked Brock because he seemed familiar to me and I was so young when we met that I did not know better. We had so much love between us and I thought if I wanted it bad enough that we could make that little white picket fence dream come true. I felt I could make it happen if I just tried hard enough. When our beautiful baby boy was born I thought Brock would come around and let go of the alcohol but he did not. The year I began Life College I ended our marriage. At 4:30 in the afternoon Brock showed up at Life College for a family get together and was obviously intoxicated. He had our son with him and I freaked out. I told him to meet me at home so we could talk because he would not drive with me. I took our son with me and drove home. Brock was not there. I went to his favorite bar near our house and there he was receiving a beer and a shot from the bartender. Done, I was done at that moment. I had asked him to get help for so long and he refused. I saw death at our door. I did not know if it would be us who perished or and innocent family but I knew if we did not leave someone was going to die. Blackness was all around my beautiful, innocent little boy and me.

I was devastated and faced with raising my son by myself with no money and determined to continue on with my education. I had to make a better life for my son, than I had growing up. My son and I had $365 coming in monthly. I found an apartment across the street from Life College that charged $350 bills included and my son and I moved in. To this day I do not know how we made it through the first eight months. I borrowed $350 from my mother at that time. She had turned her back on me when I left my husband and supported Brock through the divorce. It felt awful to even ask her for help, but I did. It took me five months but I paid my Mother back the money she loaned us. It did not stop her boyfriend, Ed, from berating me for borrowing the money a year later. It was hurtful and confusing to me why these people verbally attacked me. In their eyes I am this awful person. It is something I cannot wrap my brain around. It took me so many years to realize that I am a good person and a wonderful Mother. Growing up, being treated like dirt and made to feel like you're this horrible person is a tough chain to break. My self-esteem and self-worth were all in the hands of people that truly cannot love and it has taken me a life time to break away. I kept thinking all of those years that one day they would come around and say we are sorry. Sorry never came. What I do know as a parent is that children need and deserve your unconditional love and support. Kids need to know that you have their back through thick and thin. That is our honor as parents. To Love and nurture that beautiful little soul that has been entrusted to us.

Our apartment was in a very bad section of town and the first day we were there a young man ran by our window with a police officer hot on his trail. I yelled to my son to hit the floor because I was not sure what was going on. It turns out the young man had stolen a van and had driven up the curb in front of our apartment before taking off on foot. Gun shots were heard nightly and I was very scared for our safety. It was such a hard time for my little one and I. He missed his Dad and he missed us being together but due to life choices on both our parts his Dad and I could no longer be together. I was heartbroken for my son but in my heart I knew I was doing the right thing for our lives. While living in that scary apartment we had a close call. I was home studying for an exam and I had earplugs in because the dog next door kept barking. My four year old son was napping in my bedroom. I went to the restroom and before I knew it, Jim, a guy from school was walking toward me down the hall. I was so embarrassed and confused. I slammed the door really fast. When I walked into the living room Jim was looking at our Christmas tree. What was he doing walking into our apartment? He said, "I didn't know you were home." This was an odd statement for a trespasser. This guy was really young. He had just moved to Georgia from some little town in Maine and I thought he was just naive. I told him that people do not enter other people's homes uninvited. I had assigned seating next to Jim at school and it was awkward to sit next to him after that. I always made sure my door was locked after that day. About 4 weeks later my ex-husband was bringing my son home and I had to go to Gross Anatomy lab. We had a 10 minute span of time between me leaving and him bringing Caleb back so I left the door unlocked knowing that he would be there shortly. When I returned home there was a note in big red letters sitting on my kitchen table. It read, CHARLIE CALL ME, Jim. My heart jumped out of my chest and I asked Brock how that got on my table. He said it was there when he showed up with Caleb. Shortly after that I received a call from Jim. He asked me if I received the note. I hung up. The next day I tracked my Gross Anatomy teacher down and demanded that he move me to another seat as far away from the scary guy as I could get. I moved that day and never spoke to him again. 6 months later a friend called and said, "Charlie you have to turn on the news." There on the screen was a mug shot of Jim. It turns out this guy was an arsonist. He had started 14 fires in his apartment complex and he had burned down my college friend, Kendra's apartment. My son and I were definitely protected because there was a basement apartment below our apartment that had been vacant for 30 years. There was no door on this apartment so anyone could have gotten into this basement and set it ablaze. Even though darkness surrounded my son and I we had angelic protection. I am sure of it. I am not sure what happened to Jim. I believe his parents were trying to get him off with an insanity plea. Kendra is the one of the sweetest people I know. Just knowing how close she had come to danger turned her whole world upside down. She had been in her home town when the blaze was set but all of her belongings were gone. His parents were extremely wealthy so I am hoping they did not buy their sons freedom. He had mentioned to my friend Stan that the club house near his home had been set ablaze before moving to Georgia for school. He told Stan they never caught the person responsible. I hope they opened that case again and took a look at the evidence.

5 months later I met a very kind lady who leased apartments in a beautiful complex. She too had been a single mother and she made sure we had new paint and new carpet in our beautiful new apartment. The complex had a pool and Caleb and I played at that pool all the time. We have so many wonderful memories there. We threw all of our water toys in our wagon and rolled it to the pool. Many of my college friends lived at our complex so when we showed up the pool party began. Water gun fights, floaties, squish balls, and footballs were everywhere. Life was looking much better. We also brought home two baby kitties that I received from my little brother, Joe. We loved those babies so much. Nastasha was with us for 15 years

and Sam was with us for 17 years. They were a blessing in our lives. 0:)

My son and I made a family of two which consisted of love, peace, and joy. For the first time since the age of 4 I had tranquility in my home. I dove into spiritual books about that time and with the help of my wonderful friends at Life Chiropractic College and with the healing books a beautiful change began to occur.

In 1998 I visited The Dominican of Republic two weeks after Hurricane Georges ravaged the Island. After witnessing the devastation and the incredible strength of the Dominican people, I prayed. I said, "God I cannot help these people, I am just one person," and the creator said, "Yes you can." Now this is 9 years before Barack Obama coined those terms so I have concluded the creator must say this a lot. :) I began building Angel Boxes on the Life campus in December 1998. On the beautiful boxes we wrote that we were collecting donations for people in need in the United States, The Dominican, Columbia, Honduras, China, etc. Since 300-500 students and faculty traveled throughout the world every 3 months, each person bringing one box of goods with them and we were able to deliver over 70 tons of donations to people in need. The Angel Boxes were featured in many publications. It was an exciting time and I found a joy that my soul had never known. I also knew at that time that I had found my soul work. What I was put on this earth to do. In a nutshell it is to HELP PEOPLE. Anyway I can. With a kind word, with shoes and clothes so people can work, to heal their bodies and minds, to give them inspiration so they too can fulfill their dreams. I am here to let people know that it does not matter where you come from. As a matter of fact, use your experiences in life to show you how magnificent you really are. To show you the strength and love that resides in your heart and soul. It takes courage and not giving up. No one knows the truth of your soul better than you so let that shine and begin to dream. Write your dream. See your dream every day. Feel it, like you have already walked into it. Just feel it. You do not even have to believe it can even come true. Just PRETEND it has. Grasp the little child in you and remember how that child Pretended and Imagined. Wake that child up. That is your true essence and I see that essence in every person I meet. I see the God in you. Do you see the God in you? That is the key. You are so miraculous and beautiful. You shine so bright and it is time to take your Power back. The only thing that matters on this planet is that you remember your true spirit. Everything else will lay out in front of you and all of the sudden you just begin to live your calling. It is something that gives you joy, love, and peace. It fills you up with divine energy and you could do it all day, every day and be lost in bliss. It could be art, writing, helping people and animals, writing and producing movies, building awesome inventions, etc... This is the meaning of life. It is to find your joy, your bliss, your heaven on earth. I chose to heal. It has not been easy but I would not change it for the world. This journey I have been on since 1995 has been purely divine. I am so grateful. It does not matter where you begin today. If you choose to heal, you will. If you choose to stay it is ok. Life is free choice. We cannot choose for another person. They cannot choose for us. If you choose to heal, people around you will either back you, drop you, or test you. You may love them very much but their journey is not your journey so bless them and give them freedom to choose their path.

Life Chiropractic College was tough. Blood, sweat, and tears is how I describe it. It makes me so proud to go through a curriculum like that and succeed. If you do not give up it is impossible to fail. Words I live by. I was fighting demons from the past and trying so hard to make a future for my son and I. I realized I sabotaged myself all the time. I would be doing fantastic in my studies and then really mess up and then I would have to stress out the rest of the trimester and put myself through all kinds of hell for months on end. I just realized one day that I was making life so hard on myself. It still took years to work my way out of it. When you have been on a roller coaster your entire life it is very hard to take yourself off that roller coaster. Ok, it was hard for me. I remember cooking breakfast for my son when we had just begun living "normally." We were finally in a beautiful place and all I felt was numbness. I realized that I only felt anything when we had extreme highs and extreme lows. It was wonderful to clue into why I felt numb so much. My nervous system had been working on survival mode for over 25 years. What helped was to read books that resonated with my soul. Books that helped me heal. Laughing. Lots and lots of laughter. Good friends and writing. When I write, God writes back. I dream, God speaks to me and I get wisdom unlike anything on this earth. I pray and I am in the presence of something miraculous that I have been calling God, or the creator, or my higher self. I cannot explain it in mere words. It is all too encompassing and divine to describe. All I can say is Thank you, thank you, thank you!!!

After graduating Life Chiropractic I had my second son, Micheal. His father and I ended our relationship when I was pregnant with Micheal and it again, devastated me. I met Micheal's dad when he was 9. His name is John. I thought he was the cutest little boy I had ever seen. He had these huge dimples and smiled at me from the bottom of the staircase at my best friend's house. I was 12 and he was just a little boy to me. The next time I saw this little boy, I was walking home from the pool when I was 15 years old. My friend Grant and John whizzed up on their skateboards. I talked to the boys for a while. I did not know this was the same boy I had met before because he had changed so much in 3 years. I remember thinking as I walked away. "Aren't they cute, like salt and pepper." You see, Grant had white blond hair and John had jet black hair so they looked like salt and pepper to me. At the age of 21 I was managing a Red Lobster. My boyfriend and I had come back to our home town for a visit. We went to this wonderful Greek restaurant. We were the only two people eating there and an extremely cute cook walks out of the kitchen. I could not help but notice him. He was extremely handsome but he looked so sad. I berated myself for checking out another guy while dating someone. Well flash forward 10 years later. I am at the car wash near my childhood home. It was a warm February day and I wanted to clean my dirty car. I was at the car wash with my son Caleb waiting for the people in front of us to hurry up. I was trying very hard not to get upset because it looked like they were going to be there forever. I decided to be nice so I made small talk with them. All of the sudden I had this feeling from the center of my gut. It screamed at me. I have never had this experience again. The words I received were, "TALK TO HIM," I was shocked remember saying to myself, ok, ok, I will talk to him. What was that? I will never know but that was an incredible experience. The next afternoon we met at my favorite little sandwich shop. As I was getting out of my car the young men met me in the parking lot. One of them smiled and I said, "I have seen you before. I do not know where but I have definitely seen you before." The three of us talked about my trip to the Dominican and the angel boxes I had been creating. We all said goodbye and as I was driving back to college the following day it hit me. This was the same person I met at my friend's house when he was 9 years old. Later when he and I were dating he showed me a picture of him at 12 years old and there he was with Grant. They looked exactly the way I remember him on his skateboard. During that time he told me he had worked at the Greek restaurant near our childhood homes, when he was in high school. By this time I was just shocked. I asked him if any other young cooks worked there at that time. He told me the only other cook was the 65 year old owner. I had been recognizing him for years. My soul knows him. I cannot explain it any other way. To top it off he lived in a house visible to my family home while I was growing up so we were only 4 houses away from each other that entire time. It did not work out forever for us but we have a God given angel because of the love we shared with each other. We loved each other very deeply. That part was not a mistake. I think more than anything it was choice. I chose to fulfill my life's destiny and he chose his destiny. We are on different paths in our lives. May God Bless him on his journey.

At the time that I gave birth to Micheal I was working at my first Chiropractic job and I was faced with raising a 10 year old and a newborn on my own. Again I prayed and slowly began to heal. My friends helped me through the pregnancy and Micheal's Godmother, Marie, stayed with us for a while after Micheal was born. She was a Godsend and I am so grateful for her being there at that time. When Micheal was 1 1/2 years old I started my own Chiropractic practice. I have always been scared of doing something new but as always it worked out fine and our practice stayed in that location for three years.

In 2005 I spoke with my friend in Florida. It was January and he was on the beach in Florida. I remember thinking how wonderful it would be to feel the sun on my face and hear the waves. For years I had been telling my oldest son that I was moving the day he graduated high school and my destination was Florida, so talking to my friend encouraged me to look at my Florida Chiropractic requirements. Florida Boards stated that I would have to take my four National Boards over again and I would have to take the Florida State Boards. I could not spend that much time away from home, jetting around the country taking board reviews and board exams while raising two boys by myself and running a full time Chiropractic business so I decided to let my lifelong dream of living in Florida go. I also knew at that time that Caleb would not graduate for 5 years and that the housing market in Florida was skyrocketing. I remember thinking, even if I could make it to Florida how would I ever find affordable housing and an office to build my practice again. I sadly put my Florida file in my file cabinet where it sat for 4 more years.

In 2005 I also took a trip to Cancun, Mexico with a group of Chiropractors for Continuing Education classes. While in Mexico I tapped into something I had never realized I could do. I somehow manifested a beautiful home that the children and I lived in for the next 5 years. It included an office on the bottom two floors and living quarters on the top three floors. It was a dream come true and looking back on that time I am still in awe over that amazing experience but more on that later. :)

Jumping Off

I n 2009 I had to make a decision to stay in Idaho where it was perfectly set up to live the rest of my life comfortably or, or, or… jump off that diving board into the unknown. Caleb was going to graduate in 2010 so I had many decisions to make if I really was going to begin my life over by the seashore. After thinking it over I decided to follow my dreams of moving south near the ocean. Yes I was leaving a successful practice to begin again but I knew in my heart that I had too. Why? Because I knew if I quit living my dreams, I my soul would slowly wilt and… that is just not good enough…;). At that time I was thinking about either moving to South Carolina or Texas but I kept getting this feeling that the Florida Board requirements had changed. After 3 weeks of this hunch plaguing my psyche I finally checked the website and it stated the requirements for Chiropractic would change on 7/31/09. Chiropractors no longer had to take their 4 national boards again and Florida boards were no longer required. Now this was no small feat. This change in requirements had never happened in Florida, ever. If I had decided to chase Florida requirements in 2005 I would have spent over $20,000 and years of studying and so much time being away from my children. I knew the market had changed in Florida and that housing was affordable so I could find an inexpensive place to live as we began our new life. Caleb was graduating in June 2010 so the mountains of obstacles had miraculously evaporated and the path was open. The board's surprised me the most out of all of the changes and still mystifies me today.

For one year I went through 12 rooms and four bathrooms to clear out our beloved house and practice. We gave away and sold all of the possessions that I had been holding on to for so many years. Instead of mourning the objects that I had let go I felt like a turtle shedding its shell. It felt free and for the first time in my life I realized that the only things that really matter to me are my pictures and my son's baby items. Everything else is just stuff.

My Heaven, My Peace :)

==

We moved to Florida in July, 2010. I rented a 5ft. By 8ft. trailer and hitched it to my SUV. We packed the trailer full of a few necessities and left everything that my son Caleb needed for his first apartment. Caleb traveled to Florida with us and flew back to Idaho two weeks later so he could begin college. I had my two sons, our two dogs, our 2 cats, and a beta fish in the SUV. I felt like the Beverly Hill Billy's. It was a funny sight. We landed in Florida two days later, tired and scared. I had so much fear of the unknown. What was I doing, leaving our safe world behind and beginning again. My oldest son was very upset that I was moving to Florida. He and I had always been together. I asked him if he would consider moving with us to Florida but he wished to stay in Idaho and I respected his decision. I told him, "My home is your healing home and whenever you need a rest you come home." My youngest son Micheal, did not want to leave his friends either. This was tough on me but I felt I had this window of opportunity and that I had to move at the magical date that I had picked out when my oldest son Caleb, was only 4 years old. The day Caleb flew home was one of the saddest days I have ever had. I miss him so much. I Love You Caleb and I am So Proud of You!!:) Since Micheal did not want to leave Idaho either, I told him Florida would be fun and that we would hunt for treasure. So far he has found over 120 shark's teeth, a huge Megladon shark tooth, and a beautiful Conch shell. Word is out on the treasure but we have not given up:)

When we landed in Florida we stayed at a hotel for one month until our rental house was ready for us to move in. I did not know how long it would take to process my Chiropractic license so while I waited I had to find temporary work. I worked at the hotel that my son and I were living at our first month in Florida. They needed a maintenance person so I cleaned the outside area of the hotel and the pool for 3 weeks in August. That is an experience a Midwesterner will never forget. It was so hot that I was soaked from head to toe by 8:00 a.m. That place was sparkling though. :) I also worked as a waitress at a local restaurant. I hadn't worked as a waitress since the early 90's and it was also a workout. You see I was willing to work extremely hard to reach my goal. I could have just waited for my Chiropractic license but at that time I had no idea if it would take a year or a month to process.

I received my license 3 months later and I was so happy. I had a Chiropractic position waiting for me when I was credentialed so I began working immediately. The Chiropractor I worked for agreed to pay me a salary for a year and then I would pay him half of my income. This was a great way to build my patient base so I took this job over 6 other Chiropractic jobs that I had been offered in Florida. Four months later the Chiropractor that I worked for told me he could not afford to keep me on salary and I would be going to commission pay only. That would mean some weeks I may not get paid or possibly make $100-$200 and my son and I could not survive on that income. The awesome thing about that time was that I had been crossing over this bridge close to our house that led to an island that is truly magnificent. I had been dreaming about building a Chiropractic practice right there on the beach. I had even written about it in my journal. Why not, right. When I had been in college years earlier I told my friends that I would someday have a practice on the beach. After receiving the news that my pay was cut I promptly gave my two week notice. I rode my bike up and down the beach to find a location to place my practice I asked a business owner if I could rent a room in her salon. She graciously agreed and for 2 months I practiced out of her salon. My patients were not as happy about this situation because of the smell of hair chemicals when they walked in the door. I searched the beach again and found a little office space in a wonderful plaza not far from where I was living. I rented that space and began cleaning and painting. I had sold or given away most of my Chiropractic equipment in Idaho so I used my portable Chiropractic table and happily began working in my own space. We began this new practice with $1000 or less. How? Again, I will never know but we did it and after 2 years a much larger space became available in our plaza and I rented that space and moved the practice 50 feet closer to the ocean. :) Miraculous happenings. The new office is absolutely amazing. With the help of my artistic son we brought new colors to our current location that just makes you smile and feel hugged every time you walk in the door. I have tried to create an atmosphere in both of my beach offices that make you feel you are in a tropical oasis versus a sterile and boring doctor's office. It truly is a magical island and a magical location:) I am so very happy and grateful. My son and I live 1 block from my office so I am never far from home. I walk to work and live a very simple peaceful life here on this island. The mainland is just over the bridge and the people that live here love the tranquility so much. It has been an answer to many prayers and as I look back none of it was a mistake. I knew I wanted to live and work in Florida. I shot the arrow out and it was close to that magic bulls eye. I re-shot the arrow when I was given the notice that my pay was cut. At the time I was extremely worried about how my son and I were going to make it and it turns out that I was being given a wonderful gift. Who knew? It has taught me so much. When obstacles come at me now I sit back and think about how it can help us in our lives. It turns everything from a negative to a positive. I also practice meditation, yoga and walking the beach. I finally learned to meditate with Vianna Stabin's book, Theta Healing. It is a wonderful book and thanks to her I can finally reach a peace and understanding that I have never known before.

Through My Eyes

I have learned through many years of healing that our only "job" is to feel joy. In the book, "Zero Limit" it states there are only two human emotions, love and fear. Everything else is categorized under these two emotions. For example, Joy-Love, Anger-Fear, Peace-Love, Hate-Fear, Kindness-Love. If this is the case it is our job to heal the fear and embrace love. Sounds simple and it is when you think with your heart first. Ego loves to get in the way but when you have an important decision to make are you using your heart? Are you thinking of everyone involved? Is it fair to everyone? Would you want someone to make that kind of decision for you? You will never go wrong if you feel life through with your heart riding shotgun. It keeps life simple and beautiful. I just have to note here that it is ok at this moment if you feel that your life is way out of sync. I have been there and with only an idea and a dream I was able to make the life of my dreams. If that is the case your only job today is to begin dreaming about your perfect life. Let's say you have all the money in the world to live your dream life. Where would you be? What would you be doing? How would you feel? Who would you be sharing your dream with? That is it. Just get the feeling now and when it is time write out it out on paper. If it calls to you, keep it, burn it, or tear it up. Whatever you do with this priceless paper does not matter because the magic has already been sent out into the universe.

Here is a little story about a magical napkin :)

In 2005 I was a happy but tired single Momma, Business Owner, and Chiropractor. My friend Megan was getting ready to go on a trip with over 100 other Chiropractors to Mexico for continual education classes. Rough right? The classes were given on the plane and on the beach. Nice way to continue my education and I really needed a break. I wake up early. My oldest son taught me many years ago to be up at the break of dawn and I have not kicked that habit. I woke up before any of my friends so I relaxed in this beautiful veranda overlooking the ocean and resort pool and I wrote on a napkin, my dream life. In my dream life I had a beautiful home surrounded by woods and water with a huge yard. We had one busy road adjacent to our dream property because I had my Chiropractic practice on this property. This was a dream so I could make it anyway I wanted too. I even drew a picture of it. I felt at that very moment that anything was possible. I drew the layout of the house and every room was recorded on this napkin.

When I went back to Idaho everything, I mean everything, landed in my path perfectly. I built my dream home. I had my beloved woods, a bike trail (bonus), a beautiful lake, even 1 busy road. My children were in a neighborhood and my patients loved the quaintness and business atmosphere in the office. On our south side were houses on our north side the beautiful water. We built that 5 level healing house by way of a napkin. Our healing house is close to my heart and it not only sheltered, loved, and fed us for 4 years it has also served as a stair step to the way of the divine. Even though you may not be on vacation when you write about your dream life it is important to pick a nice private place to write. Whether it is on your couch snuggled up with a cup of tea or coffee, in nature, museum, church, or art gallery. Whatever brings you peace and joy will be a perfect place to bring forth the energy of the universe that is waiting to connect with your spirit. While you're at it consider how you dream of seeing the world because this too helps the entire world. Energy is palpable and it travels worldwide. Isn't that miraculous? What does your heaven look like? I moved to Florida to live my heaven on earth. After moving to the most awesome little beach town in the world I am finally home. People are happy on the beach. It is easy to live blissfully here. We are so blessed. Through my eyes, this world is absolutely amazing, beautiful, loving, and most all, fun. You may be thinking, wait a minute Charlie, I see how horrible this world is because of negative news. Well does the news tell you about the billions of people that are fed every day? I see random acts of kindness that is in every city, every neighborhood, every school, church, workplace, etc. Love, forgiveness, joy, generosity, kindness, and empathy have made the roots of this country very strong and it is still here today. This is what I see. We are a nation of people that are strong and noble and the distant past and not so distant past has made us even more united. We, the American people are the United States. Decide right now if you are going to go for what you know in your heart is a fantastic life. Life is made to be exciting, an adventure, learning, loving, and giving. It does not matter how you pick your life to be it just matters that you go with your own heart. This is where joy lives. Have fun with it. Once your dreams take breath they have life. The universe and you are now on the same page and as partners in life you will create MAGIC. In the word imagine is I AM A GINE. I am a genie. When you use your imagination, you are your own genie and you grant yourself your own wish. You are a partner in this entire process and the universe will sweep you up and bring you exactly where you dream of going.

Another nudge from the universe lately has had me thinking about the way I work out. I walk the beaches, walk my awesome dogs, lift weights, and try to fit in yoga when I have time. I have felt the need to nurture my body and spirit more through yoga and walking. Lifting weights is great but my body is just letting me know that right now it needs nurturing. I suppose I have had nudges before and now I am actually more in tune and listening to the whisper of my soul. It has been fun because I look at my work schedule and plan my week with yoga as one of the main objectives. By the way, I happen to love yoga so I am at peace with myself knowing I am not abusing myself to get healthier. In my past I have put myself in pain to work out and now I am just allowing my body to communicate and tell me what it needs. I am now excited about going to the gym and working out. The walks on the beach are always magical. The beach is 1 block from my home so I walk on the beach as much as possible. My goal is to walk at least 30 minutes a day.

Two weeks ago I walked the beach around 10:00 a.m. A dolphin decided to join me and I was thrilled. I thought it was just traveling up the coast to meet up with its family but I was amazed when I stopped and the dolphin circled around and headed toward me. I was standing on the beach with my feet in the water and I stood there watching this beautiful and playful dolphin. It raised its head as if to say hi, turned around and swam back to deeper water. Eventually it met up with another dolphin and they played in front of me. It was a happy day. The two dolphins followed me up the beach and swam toward me at times and then swam to deeper water. What amazed me the most is that when I stopped, they stopped also. When I began walking, they began swimming in the same direction at the same pace. I love animals and I especially love dolphins. I literally had the new experience of walking with dolphins. It was a magical day.

As I walk the beaches I pray the entire time. I feel very connected to the ocean and the animal life in the ocean and every time I pray and touch the water with my feet I feel a healing taking place. It took me 43 years to reach this beautiful paradise on earth and I am so grateful and humbled to be here. All I can say is thank you, thank you, thank you.

I am sharing my story so the billions of people who have been told that they will never amount to anything because of the poverty or abuse they may have been born into, bad grades, no college education, etc… this book is for you because I am here to tell you that you have in you everything you need to live the life you have always envisioned. It is waiting for you. Say thank you and good bye to your past and embrace this moment and revel in this very moment. You have the power in you to create your dream life. See how strong you really are because you're a living example of incredible strength, love, and wisdom. Put a picture on your wall of your dream life so you see it every morning and you will be amazed at what transforms.

Dive in and "Heal thyself first." I was scheduled to be a casualty. I refused ;) Welcome to my beautiful life. It has been one exhilarating and miraculous ride and I am just beginning. This is the Ho'oponopono prayer I say when I am in fear, "I Love You, I am Sorry, Please Forgive me, Thank You. :)" This heals the fear coming in and neutralizes the energy into pure and divine Love. Today give yourself permission to live the life you dream about and it is yours.

Right when I am ready to get this healing book out to the public something magical happens and I have to include it in here. Last week I received a package from Harpo Studios. Well as you all probably know this is Oprah Winfrey's studio in Chicago, Illinois. I opened it and inside was an 8 by 10 inch picture of Oprah. She wrote, "Dr. Charlie, Many Blessings, Oprah Winfrey." It completely floored me. I had written the Obamas, Biden, and Oprah about the push for Chiropractors to prescribe drugs, (which I am completely opposed to) and I thought that she signed photos to everyone that wrote her. I also thought that she was one busy lady to do all of that signing. Well my friend Lewis called the next day and said, "I see you received your picture." All of the sudden the pieces fell together and I laughed and said, "Lewis you're behind this, thank you, thank you, thank you." You see my friend Lewis is friends with Stedman and Oprah. He spent the holidays with them in New Jersey and asked them to please sign a picture for his friend and Chiropractor, Charlie. They graciously agreed and now Oprah adorns my front door and blesses my practice. Thank you Oprah, Thank you Stedman, and Thank you Lewis!!!! You all ROCK:) I know this is just a quiet nudge from the universe and maybe even Oprah saying, keep going, you're on the right path. Keep the faith:) I am truly blessed.

About the Author

I live in a little beach town in Florida with my youngest son. He is my artist and I have his work displayed at my Chiropractic office. I tell Micheal all of the time he is the World's Greatest Artist:) My oldest son, Caleb, is in college in Idaho, studying film. He is so happy to be pursuing his dreams. It is his passion, his play, and his love. He is already tapping into the divine and his life is a beautiful example of joy on earth. Both of my children have been taught to follow their bliss and they are doing just that. I am so very proud of them. My children are most definitely Angels. They saved my life and have given me more joy and love then I have ever encountered on this earth. I treasure then and feel so blessed to be their Momma. I have changed the names of my family and friends to honor their privacy. The information is correct but locations have also been changed to provide privacy for the parties involved. Thank you for understanding and may you be blessed with Peace, Abundance, Laughter, Joy, Freedom, and most of all, Love ☺

Charlie De La Cruz